YOU

VS

BOUNDARIES

A Step-By-Step Guide to Setting Healthy Boundaries to Take Control of Your Life

By: Dominic Cooper

This guide is dedicated to my wonderful and resilient mother.

Contents

Introduction

Welcome to "You vs Boundaries: A Step-By-Step Guide to Setting Healthy Boundaries to Take Control of Your Life."

In this book, we will explore the importance of boundaries and how to set and maintain them in various areas of your life. Boundaries are essentially the limits we set for ourselves in terms of what we are and are not willing to tolerate or allow in our lives. These limits can be physical, emotional, or psychological and can be set in various areas of our lives, including work, relationships, and personal time.

Setting boundaries is an important aspect of self-care and is necessary for maintaining healthy relationships and overall well-being. When we have clear boundaries, we are able to protect ourselves from being taken advantage of or being subjected to harmful or abusive behaviors. We are also able to communicate our needs and expectations to others, which can help to prevent misunderstandings and conflicts.

However, setting boundaries can be challenging for some people, especially if they have a history of people-pleasing or if they struggle with low self-esteem. In this book, we will discuss common barriers to setting boundaries and provide strategies for overcoming them. We will also discuss the importance of self-awareness, assertiveness, and learning to say "no" in setting and maintaining boundaries.

By the end of this book, you will have a better understanding of the importance of boundaries and how to set and maintain them in your own life. We hope that you find this guide helpful in your journey towards self-care and healthy relationships.

Importance of Setting Boundaries

Boundaries are an important aspect of self-care and are necessary for maintaining healthy relationships and overall well-being. Boundaries are essentially the limits we set for ourselves in terms of what we are and are not willing to tolerate or allow in our lives. These limits can be physical, emotional, or psychological and can be set in various areas of our lives, including work, relationships, and personal time.

There are several reasons why setting boundaries is important. First and foremost, boundaries help to protect our physical, emotional, and psychological well-being. When we have clear boundaries, we are better able to protect ourselves from being taken advantage of or being subjected to harmful or abusive behaviors. For example, if we have a boundary in place that says we will not tolerate physical abuse in a relationship, we are able to remove ourselves from a potentially dangerous situation.

Boundaries are also important for maintaining healthy relationships. When we have clear boundaries, we are able to communicate our needs and expectations to others, which can help to prevent misunderstandings and conflicts. For example, if we have a boundary that says we need alone time to recharge after a long day, we can communicate this to our partner and they can respect our need for space.

In addition to protecting our well-being and maintaining healthy relationships, boundaries are also necessary for maintaining our sense of self. When we have clear boundaries, we are better able to assert our needs and desires, which can help us to feel more confident and in control of our lives. Without clear boundaries, we may find ourselves feeling overwhelmed or taken for granted by others.

However, setting boundaries can be challenging for some people, especially if they have a history of people-pleasing or if they struggle with low self-esteem. Some common barriers to setting boundaries include fear of rejection, fear of conflict, and feelings of guilt. It's important to recognize and address these barriers in order to effectively set boundaries in our lives.

One way to overcome these barriers is to practice self-awareness. This involves becoming more aware of our own thoughts, feelings, and needs. When we are self-aware, we are better able to identify and communicate our boundaries to others. It's also helpful to practice assertiveness, which involves standing up for ourselves and expressing our needs and desires in a clear and respectful way.

Another key aspect of setting boundaries is learning to say "no." This can be difficult for some people, especially if they are used to putting the needs of others before their own. However, it's important to remember that it's okay to say "no" and that it's not necessary to always be available to others. Saying "no" can be a powerful way to set boundaries and assert our own needs.

It's also important to remember that boundaries are not meant to be rigid or inflexible. They can and should be adjusted as our needs and circumstances change. For example, if we have a boundary that says we need alone time after work, we may be able to relax this boundary on the weekends if we have other plans.

In conclusion, setting boundaries is an important aspect of self-care and is necessary for maintaining healthy relationships and overall well-being. By practicing self-awareness, assertiveness, and learning to say "no," we can effectively set and maintain boundaries in our lives. Remember that boundaries can and should be adjusted as needed and that it's okay to prioritize our own needs and desires.

Step 1
Identify Your Needs and Values

The first step in setting boundaries is to become aware of your own needs and values. Take some time to reflect on what is important to you and what you need in order to feel healthy and happy.

Here are some steps to help you identify your needs and values:

1. Reflect on your past experiences: Think about times in your life when you felt fulfilled, satisfied, and happy. What were you doing in those moments? What did you value about those experiences? Reflecting on your past experiences can give you clues about what you need and value in your life.

2. Take some time for self-exploration: Set aside some time to really focus on what you want and need in your life. This can be done through activities such as journaling, meditation, or talking with a trusted friend or therapist.

3. Consider your core values: Your values are the things that are most important to you and shape your beliefs and actions. Some common values include honesty, loyalty, family, and personal growth. Take some time to think about what values are most important to you and how they influence your decisions.

4. Identify your physical and emotional needs: Your needs are the things that you require in order to feel healthy and satisfied. These can include physical needs such as rest and nutrition, as well as emotional needs such as love, connection, and security. Take some time to think about what your physical and emotional needs are and how you can meet them.

5. Be honest with yourself: It's important to be honest with yourself about what you need and value in your life. Don't be afraid to acknowledge your own desires and to set boundaries that reflect your needs and values.

Identifying your needs and values can be a challenging but rewarding process. It may take time and self-exploration to fully understand what you need and value in your life. Remember to be patient with yourself and to celebrate your progress as you work towards a life that is fulfilling and authentic.

Here are a few examples of people who recognize their needs and values:

1. A woman who prioritizes self-care and makes time for regular exercise and meditation to nourish her body and mind.

2. A man who values honesty and integrity and makes decisions that align with these values, even if they are difficult or unpopular.

3. A couple who values family and makes time for regular family dinners and vacations to strengthen their relationships and bond.

4. A person who values personal growth and takes the time to pursue education and learning opportunities to develop new skills and knowledge.

5. A person who values connection and makes an effort to cultivate meaningful relationships with friends and loved ones.

These individuals are able to recognize their needs and values and make choices that reflect and support them. By doing so, they are able to live a fulfilling and authentic life.

Identifying your needs and values is an important step in personal development and can help you lead a more fulfilling and meaningful life. Your needs and values are the things that are most important to you and shape your behavior and decision-making. They give you a sense of direction and purpose and help you prioritize your time and energy.

When you are clear about your needs and values, you are more likely to make decisions that align with them and bring you closer to your goals. This can help you feel more grounded, confident, and satisfied with your choices. On the other hand, when you are unclear about your needs and values or when they are not in alignment with your actions, you may feel conflicted, unfulfilled, or disconnected from your sense of self.

There are many ways to identify your needs and values. One effective method is to take some time to reflect on your experiences and feelings. What are the things that bring you joy, fulfillment, and meaning? What are the things that cause you stress, frustration, or discomfort? What are the things that are non-negotiable for you? This can help you gain insight into what is most important to you and what you need to feel satisfied and fulfilled in your life.

Another way to identify your needs and values is to consider your personal and professional goals. What do you want to achieve in your life? What are your long-term aspirations? Your goals can provide clues about your needs and values and help you determine what steps you need to take to move closer to them.

It is also helpful to seek the input of others, such as friends, family, or a therapist. They may have insights into your needs and values that you have not yet considered.

Once you have identified your needs and values, it is important to regularly check in with yourself to ensure that your actions are aligned with them. This can help you stay true to yourself and make choices that are authentic and meaningful to you.

In summary, identifying your needs and values is a crucial step in personal development. It can help you make informed decisions, feel more fulfilled and satisfied, and lead a more meaningful and authentic life.

Tips to Put the Steps into Practice:

Reflect on your past experiences:

1. Journaling: Writing about your experiences can be a helpful way to process your thoughts and feelings. You can try writing

about specific events or about your overall feelings and insights.

2. Talking to someone: Sharing your experiences with someone you trust, such as a friend, family member, or therapist, can be a helpful way to reflect on them. They may be able to provide a different perspective or offer support and guidance.

3. Using a reflection prompts: There are many reflection prompts that you can use to help guide your reflection. Some examples might include: "What did I learn from this experience?" or "How did this experience make me feel and why?"

4. Thinking about what you would do differently: Reflecting on what you would do differently if you could go back to a past experience can help you gain insight into your actions and behaviors.

5. Engaging in mindfulness: Mindfulness is the practice of focusing your attention on the present moment without judgment. It can be helpful for reflecting on your past experiences because it allows you to observe your thoughts and feelings without getting caught up in them.

Take some time for self-exploration:

1. Journaling: Writing down your thoughts and feelings can be a powerful tool for self-exploration. It can help you gain clarity on your thoughts and emotions and identify patterns and trends in your behavior.

2. Meditation: Meditation is a practice that involves focusing your attention on the present moment. It can help you become more aware of your thoughts and feelings and gain a greater sense of clarity and insight.

3. Therapy: Working with a therapist can be a helpful way to explore your thoughts and feelings in a safe and supportive

environment. A therapist can provide guidance and support as you work through challenging emotions and behaviors.

4. Engaging in self-care activities: Self-care activities, such as exercise, hobbies, or spending time in nature, can help you relax and clear your mind, making it easier to reflect on your thoughts and emotions.

Consider your core values:

1. Consider your goals: What are your long-term goals and aspirations? What values do they reflect? For example, if your goal is to have a successful career, this may reflect your value of achievement and ambition.

2. Reflect on your relationships: What are the most important qualities that you look for in a partner or friend? These qualities may reflect your core values.

3. Seek feedback from others: Ask friends, family members, or a therapist for their perspective on what your core values are. This can provide a different perspective and help you gain a more well-rounded understanding of your values.

4. Engage in mindfulness activities: Mindfulness practices, such as meditation or journaling, can help you gain insight into your thoughts, feelings, and values.

Identify your physical and emotional needs:

1. Pay attention to your body: Your body can provide important clues about your physical and emotional needs. Pay attention to your hunger, thirst, fatigue, and physical discomfort. These signals can indicate that you need to take care of your basic needs, such as eating, drinking, sleeping, and moving your body.

2. Notice your emotions: Emotions can provide valuable information about your needs and values. Pay attention to your feelings and try to identify what might be causing them. For example, if you are feeling anxious, you might need more time to relax and de-stress. If you are feeling angry, you might need to assert your boundaries or find a healthy outlet for your emotions.

3. Reflect on your values and priorities: Think about what is most important to you and what you need in order to feel fulfilled and satisfied. This can help you identify your emotional needs and guide your decision-making.

4. Seek feedback: Ask for feedback from others about your behavior and how you come across. This can help you gain a more accurate understanding of your needs and how you are perceived by others.

Be honest with yourself:

1. Reflect on your thoughts and feelings: Take some time to think about your thoughts and feelings and how they influence your actions and decisions. Be honest with yourself about what you are feeling and why.

2. Seek feedback from others: Ask for feedback from trusted friends, family members, or colleagues about your behavior and how you come across. Listen to what they have to say and be open to hearing things you may not want to hear.

3. Practice mindfulness: Mindfulness is the practice of focusing your attention on the present moment without judgment. It can help you become more aware of your thoughts, feelings, and sensations. By practicing mindfulness, you can gain greater insight into your own thoughts and emotions.

4. Seek support: If you are struggling with honesty, consider seeking support from a therapist or coach. They can help you gain insight into your thoughts and behaviors and provide guidance on how to be more honest with yourself.

5. Set goals and track your progress: Setting goals can help you focus on areas of your life where you want to improve. Tracking your progress can help you become more aware of your habits and patterns and be honest with yourself about where you need to make changes.

Step 2

Communicate Your Boundaries Clearly

Once you have a clear understanding of your values and needs, it's important to communicate your boundaries to others. This may involve saying no to requests or setting limits on how you spend your time and energy. Be assertive and direct, but also try to be respectful and understanding of others' perspectives.

Effective communication is key to setting boundaries in a healthy and respectful way. Here are some tips for communicating your boundaries clearly:

1. Use "I" statements: Instead of saying "You shouldn't do that," try saying "I feel uncomfortable when you do that." This helps to make it clear that you are expressing your own feelings and boundaries, rather than trying to control the other person.

2. Be specific: Clearly articulate what your boundary is and what behaviors or actions are not acceptable. For example, instead of saying "I don't like it when you invade my privacy," try saying "I have a boundary around not having my phone or

emails checked without my permission. It's important to me that we respect each other's privacy."

3. Be assertive: It's important to stand up for yourself and be clear about your boundaries. This may involve saying no to requests or setting limits on your time and energy. At the same time, try to be respectful and understanding of others' perspectives.

4. Practice active listening: When setting boundaries with others, it's important to listen to their perspective and try to understand where they are coming from. This can help to build trust and strengthen your relationship.

5. Use nonverbal communication: Body language, tone of voice, and facial expressions can all convey important information. Make sure that your nonverbal communication is consistent with your verbal communication and reflects the boundaries you are trying to set.

6. Be open to negotiation: While it's important to stand up for your boundaries, it's also important to be open to negotiation and compromise. Try to find a solution that works for both you and the other person.

By following these tips, you can communicate your boundaries clearly and effectively, helping to create healthy and respectful relationships.

Here are some examples of people who communicate their boundaries clearly to live a more fulfilling life:

1. A person who has a boundary around not working overtime on weeknights communicates this boundary to their boss and colleagues. They explain that they value their personal time and need to have a work-life balance.

2. A person who has a boundary around not discussing their private life with coworkers communicates this boundary to

their colleagues. They explain that they value their privacy and prefer to keep their personal life separate from their work life.

3. A person who has a boundary around not engaging in gossip communicates this boundary to their friends. They explain that they value honesty and respect and prefer to focus on positive and constructive communication.

4. A person who has a boundary around not lending money to friends communicates this boundary to their friends. They explain that they value their financial stability and prefer to avoid putting themselves in a potentially uncomfortable or difficult situation.

By communicating their boundaries clearly, these people are able to set limits and create healthy, fulfilling relationships with others. Setting boundaries can help you feel more in control of your life and relationships, and can contribute to your overall well-being and happiness.

Communicating your boundaries clearly is an essential part of maintaining healthy and respectful relationships. Boundaries are the limits we set for ourselves and others in order to protect our physical, emotional, and mental well-being. When we communicate our boundaries clearly, we are able to assert ourselves and establish healthy relationships based on mutual respect.

One of the key benefits of communicating your boundaries clearly is that it helps you feel more in control of your life and relationships. By setting limits and expressing your needs and values, you are able to create a sense of balance and autonomy. This can lead to greater feelings of self-worth and confidence, and can help you feel more fulfilled and satisfied in your relationships.

Another important reason to communicate your boundaries clearly is to avoid misunderstandings and conflict. When we are unclear about our boundaries, others may inadvertently cross them, which can lead to misunderstandings and hurt feelings. By communicating your boundaries clearly, you can help to prevent misunderstandings and reduce the potential for conflict.

Effective communication is key to setting boundaries clearly. This may involve using "I" statements to express your own feelings and needs, being specific about what behaviors or actions are not acceptable, and being assertive but respectful in your communication. It's also important to practice active listening and be open to negotiation and compromise.

In conclusion, communicating your boundaries clearly is an important part of maintaining healthy and respectful relationships. It helps you feel more in control of your life and relationships, can prevent misunderstandings and conflict, and can contribute to your overall well-being and happiness. By setting and communicating your boundaries clearly, you can create fulfilling and satisfying relationships with others.

Tips to Put the Steps into Practice:

Use "I" statements:

1. Express your own feelings: Instead of saying "You're making me angry," try saying "I feel angry when you do that." This helps to make it clear that you are expressing your own feelings, rather than trying to blame the other person.

2. Describe the behavior that is causing your feelings: Instead of saying "I feel hurt when you do that," try saying "I feel hurt when you ignore me when I'm talking." This helps to make it clear what specific behavior is causing your feelings.

3. Explain the impact of the behavior on you: Instead of saying "I feel disrespected when you do that," try saying "I feel disrespected when you interrupt me, because it makes me feel like my thoughts and opinions don't matter." This helps to

explain the impact of the behavior on you and can help the other person understand your perspective.

4. Make a request: Instead of saying "I feel frustrated when you do that," try saying "I feel frustrated when you do that. Can you please stop interrupting me when I'm speaking?" This helps to clearly express your feelings and make a request for a specific change in behavior.

Be specific:

1. Identify the specific behavior or action that is not acceptable: Instead of saying "I don't like it when you invade my privacy," try saying "I have a boundary around not having my phone or emails checked without my permission. It's important to me that we respect each other's privacy." This makes it clear what behavior is not acceptable and why it is important to you.

2. Set specific limits: Instead of saying "I don't have time for any more commitments," try saying "I can only commit to one extra project per month. It's important to me to maintain a healthy work-life balance." This helps to set a clear limit and explains why this is important to you.

3. Use specific examples: If you have a boundary around a certain behavior, it can be helpful to provide specific examples of when this boundary has been violated. For example, instead of saying "You always interrupt me," try saying "I feel disrespected when you interrupt me, like when you interrupted me during the meeting last week." This helps to make your boundary clear and provides concrete examples of when it has been violated.

Be assertive:

1. Be direct: Be clear and specific about what you want or need. Avoid beating around the bush or being vague.

2. Stand up for yourself: It's important to be assertive and stand up for yourself when necessary. This may involve saying "no" to requests or setting limits on your time and energy.

3. Use nonverbal communication: Body language, tone of voice, and facial expressions can all convey important information. Make sure that your nonverbal communication is consistent with your verbal communication and reflects your assertiveness.

4. Be open to negotiation: While it's important to stand up for yourself, it's also important to be open to negotiation and compromise. Try to find a solution that works for both you and the other person.

Practice active listening:

1. Pay attention: Give the person your undivided attention and avoid distractions such as looking at your phone or checking your emails.

2. Reflect back what you hear: Repeat back to the person what you have heard them say to confirm your understanding. For example, you could say "So what I'm hearing is that you are feeling frustrated because your boss is not recognizing your hard work."

3. Ask questions: Ask open-ended questions to clarify what the person is saying and show that you are interested in their perspective. For example, you could say "Can you tell me more about how you feel in this situation?"

4. Avoid interrupting: Allow the person to speak without interrupting them. Interrupting can come across as disrespectful and can prevent the person from fully expressing themselves.

5. Empathize: Try to understand the person's perspective and show empathy by acknowledging their feelings. For example, you could say "I can see how that would be frustrating for you."

Use nonverbal communication:

1. Use eye contact: Eye contact is a powerful way to convey interest, confidence, and attentiveness. When speaking with someone, try to make eye contact and hold it for a few seconds at a time.

2. Pay attention to your body language: Your body language can reveal a lot about your thoughts and feelings. For example, crossed arms may indicate that you are closed off or defensive, while open body language, such as uncrossed arms and facing the person directly, may indicate that you are open and receptive.

3. Use facial expressions: Facial expressions can convey a wide range of emotions, from happiness and anger to sadness and fear. Pay attention to your own facial expressions and try to match them to your words and intentions.

4. Use gestures: Gestures can be a powerful way to emphasize your words and convey meaning. For example, a hand gesture may indicate that you are making a point or asking a question.

5. Use touch: Touch can be a powerful way to convey affection, comfort, and support. However, it's important to be mindful of the other person's boundaries and only use touch if it is welcomed.

Be open to negotiation:

1. Communicate your needs and values clearly: Before entering into a negotiation, it's important to have a clear understanding of your own needs and values. This will help you know what you are willing to compromise on and what is non-negotiable.

2. Listen to the other person's perspective: It's important to listen to the other person's perspective and try to understand where they are coming from. This can help to build trust and strengthen the relationship.

3. Find common ground: Look for areas where you can find common ground and come to a mutually beneficial solution.

4. Be willing to compromise: Recognize that negotiation often involves give and take. Be willing to make concessions in order to find a solution that works for both parties.

5. Be open to alternative solutions: If a direct negotiation is not successful, consider looking for alternative solutions that might work for both parties. For example, if you are unable to come to an agreement on a specific request, you might be able to find a different way to meet each other's needs.

Step 3

Practice Self-Awareness

Pay attention to your own feelings and needs. If you find that you are feeling overwhelmed or taken advantage of, it may be a sign that you need to set a boundary.

Self-awareness is the ability to recognize and understand your own thoughts, feelings, and behaviors. It's an important skill for maintaining emotional well-being and making healthy choices. Here is a guide on how to practice self-awareness:

1. Observe your thoughts and feelings: Pay attention to your thoughts and feelings as they arise. Notice what triggers these thoughts and feelings, and how they affect your behavior.

2. Practice mindfulness: Mindfulness is the practice of focusing your attention on the present moment without judgment. It can help you become more aware of your thoughts, feelings, and sensations. You can practice mindfulness through activities such as meditation, yoga, or simply paying attention to your breath and surroundings.

3. Reflect on your actions: Take some time to reflect on your actions and behaviors. Think about why you did what you did and how it made you feel. This can help you understand your motivations and patterns of behavior.

4. Seek feedback: Ask for feedback from others about your behavior and how you come across. This can help you gain a more accurate understanding of how you are perceived by others.

5. Set goals and track your progress: Setting goals can help you focus on areas of your life where you want to improve. Tracking your progress can help you become more aware of your habits and patterns.

6. Seek support: If you are struggling with self-awareness, consider seeking support from a therapist or coach. They can help you gain insight into your thoughts and behaviors and provide guidance on how to make positive changes.

By following these steps, you can practice self-awareness and gain a better understanding of yourself and your actions. This can help you make healthier choices and improve your emotional well-being.

Here are some examples of people who practice self-awareness:

1. A person who takes time to reflect on their thoughts and feelings before making a decision. They consider how their emotions might be influencing their judgment and try to make choices that are based on reason and logic.

2. A person who engages in mindfulness activities, such as meditation or yoga, to help them stay present and aware of their thoughts and emotions.

3. A person who seeks feedback from others about their behavior and how they come across. They use this feedback to gain a better understanding of their strengths and weaknesses and work on areas for improvement.

4. A person who sets goals for themselves and tracks their progress. They use this process to become more aware of their habits and patterns and make changes as needed.

5. A person who seeks support from a therapist or coach to help them gain insight into their thoughts and behaviors. They use this support to make positive changes in their life.

By practicing self-awareness, these people are able to gain a better understanding of themselves and their actions. This can help them make healthier choices and improve their emotional well-being.

Self-awareness is the ability to recognize and understand your own thoughts, feelings, and behaviors. It's an important skill for maintaining emotional well-being and making healthy choices. Self-awareness also plays a crucial role in setting boundaries, as it allows you to identify your values and needs and communicate them to others.

One of the key benefits of self-awareness is that it helps you understand your own feelings and needs. By being attuned to your emotions, you can identify when you are feeling overwhelmed or taken advantage of, which can be a sign that you need to set a boundary. Self-awareness can also help you identify your values and prioritize what is most important to you, which can inform the boundaries you set.

Effective communication is an important part of setting boundaries, and self-awareness can help you communicate your boundaries clearly and assertively. By being aware of your own feelings and needs, you can use "I" statements to express your boundaries in a clear and respectful way.

Self-awareness can also help you be more flexible and open to negotiation when it comes to setting boundaries. By understanding your own motivations and needs, you can be open to adjusting your boundaries when necessary, such as when a deadline comes up that requires you to work on a day you had previously set as a boundary.

In conclusion, self-awareness is an important skill for setting boundaries and maintaining healthy relationships. It allows you to identify your values and needs, communicate your boundaries clearly, and be flexible and open to negotiation. By practicing self-awareness, you can create fulfilling and satisfying relationships based on mutual respect.

Tips to Put the Steps into Practice:

Observe your thoughts and feelings:

1. Pay attention to your internal dialogue: Notice the thoughts that come up in your mind throughout the day. What are you telling yourself about yourself, others, and the world around you?

2. Notice your emotional reactions: Pay attention to your emotional reactions to different situations. What triggers these reactions and how do they affect your behavior?

3. Reflect on your actions: Take some time to reflect on your actions and behaviors. Think about why you did what you did and how it made you feel. This can help you understand your motivations and patterns of behavior.

Practice mindfulness:

1. Meditation: Meditation involves sitting quietly and focusing your attention on your breath, a mantra, or an object. It can help you quiet your mind and become more present.

2. Yoga: Yoga involves physical postures, breathing techniques, and mindfulness practices. It can help you become more attuned to your body and mind.

3. Mindful breathing: You can practice mindfulness through focused breathing exercises. Simply sit quietly and focus your attention on your breath, noticing the sensation of the air as it enters and exits your body.

4. Mindful movement: You can also practice mindfulness through movement, such as walking or dancing. Pay attention to your body and the sensations you are experiencing as you move.

5. Mindful eating: Eating can be a great opportunity to practice mindfulness. Pay attention to the sights, smells, and flavors of your food, and try to eat slowly and savor each bite.

6. Daily mindfulness practices: You can also incorporate mindfulness into your daily activities, such as showering, brushing your teeth, or going for a walk. Pay attention to your senses and the present moment as you go about your day.

Reflect on your actions:

1. Keep a journal: Write down your thoughts and feelings about your actions and behaviors. This can help you gain insight into your motivations and patterns of behavior.

2. Talk to someone: Share your thoughts and feelings with a trusted friend, family member, or therapist. They can offer a different perspective and help you gain insight into your actions.

3. Ask for feedback: Seek feedback from others about your actions and behaviors. This can help you gain a more accurate understanding of how you are perceived by others.

4. Take a step back: Sometimes it can be helpful to take a break and distance yourself from a situation in order to reflect on your actions. This can give you some perspective and help you gain clarity.

Seek feedback:

1. Ask for specific feedback: When asking for feedback, try to be specific about what you are looking for. For example, you might ask for feedback on your communication style or your time management skills.

2. Choose the right person: It's important to choose someone who you trust and who has the knowledge and experience to give you useful feedback. This might be a mentor, a colleague, or a supervisor.

3. Schedule a dedicated time: Set aside a specific time to meet with the person and ask for feedback. This will help ensure that you have their undivided attention and that they are prepared to give you quality feedback.

4. Prepare to listen: When seeking feedback, it's important to be open and receptive to what the other person has to say. Practice active listening by focusing on what they are saying and avoiding interrupting or getting defensive.

5. Follow up: After receiving feedback, take some time to reflect on it and consider how you can incorporate it into your life. If you have any questions or need clarification, don't hesitate to follow up with the person who gave you the feedback.

Set goals and track your progress:

1. Identify your goals: Start by thinking about what you want to achieve. What are your long-term goals? What are your short-term goals? What are your personal, professional, and financial goals?

2. Make your goals specific and achievable: It's important to make your goals specific and achievable. Instead of setting a vague goal like "lose weight," try setting a specific goal like "lose 10 pounds in the next three months by exercising at least three times a week and eating a healthy diet."

3. Create a plan: Once you have identified your goals, create a plan for how you will achieve them. Break your goals down into smaller, actionable steps.

4. Set deadlines: Setting deadlines can help you stay motivated and on track. Choose deadlines that are realistic, but also challenge you to make progress.

5. Track your progress: It's important to track your progress in order to stay motivated and on track. This can involve keeping a journal, using a goal-tracking app, or simply checking in with yourself regularly to assess your progress.

6. Celebrate your victories: It's important to celebrate your victories along the way. This can help you stay motivated and recognize your progress.

Seek support:

1. Talk to a trusted friend or family member: Sharing your thoughts and feelings with someone you trust can help you feel heard and understood, and can provide a sense of connection and support.

2. Seek the support of a therapist or counselor: A mental health professional can provide a safe and confidential space for you to explore your thoughts, feelings, and behaviors and help you develop coping strategies and skills for setting healthy boundaries.

3. Join a support group: Connecting with others who are facing similar challenges can be a source of support and encouragement. You can find support groups in your local community or online, on platforms such as Meetup or Facebook.

4. Seek the support of a coach or mentor: A coach or mentor can provide guidance and support as you work on setting boundaries and making positive changes in your life.

5. Seek the support of a spiritual advisor: If you have a spiritual or religious practice, you may find support and guidance through a spiritual advisor or faith community.

Step 4
Practice Saying "No"

It's okay to say no to requests or invitations that do not align with your boundaries or values. It's important to respect your own needs and boundaries, even if it means disappointing others.

Here are some tricks you can use to practice saying "no" to things you don't want to do:

1. Use "I" statements: Instead of saying "No, I can't do that," try saying "I'm sorry, but I don't feel comfortable doing that." This helps to make it clear that you are expressing your own feelings and boundaries, rather than trying to control the other person.

2. Offer an alternative solution: If you don't want to do something, but you don't want to completely shut the other person down, you can try offering an alternative solution. For example, instead of saying "No, I can't work on the weekend," you could say "I can't work on the weekend, but I could work a little extra on Wednesday evening to make up for it."

3. Set limits on your time and energy: If you find that you are frequently being asked to do things that you don't want to do, try setting limits on your time and energy. For example, you could say "I'm sorry, but I can only commit to one extra project per month."

4. Use a script: If you struggle with saying "no" in the moment, you can try using a script to help you. For example, you could say something like "I understand that this is important to you, but I have to prioritize my own well-being and I'm unable to take on any additional commitments at this time."

5. Practice saying "no" in low-stakes situations: If you are new to saying "no," it can be helpful to practice in low-stakes

situations. For example, you could practice saying "no" to a friend who asks you to go out when you're feeling tired, or to a colleague who asks you to cover their shift when you have plans.

By using these tricks, you can practice saying "no" in a respectful and assertive way, which can help you set healthy boundaries and maintain your well-being.

Here are some examples of people who say "no" to things they don't want to do:

1. A person who says "no" to attending a social event that they are not interested in. They recognize that their time and energy are valuable and choose to spend them on activities that are meaningful and enjoyable to them.

2. A person who says "no" to taking on an additional project at work when they are already feeling overwhelmed. They recognize that their well-being is important and prioritize their own needs.

3. A person who says "no" to a friend who asks them to lend them money. They have a boundary around not lending money to friends and communicate this boundary clearly.

4. A person who says "no" to a colleague who asks them to cover their shift when they have plans. They recognize that they have a right to their own time and prioritize their own commitments.

By saying "no" to things they don't want to do, these people are able to set healthy boundaries and prioritize their own needs and well-being. This can help them feel more in control of their lives and relationships.

Saying "no" can be a difficult but important skill for setting boundaries and maintaining your well-being. It's natural to want to please others and avoid conflict, but constantly saying "yes" to things you don't want to do can lead to feelings of overwhelm and resentment. By learning to say "no" and setting healthy boundaries, you can take control of your life and prioritize your own needs and well-being.

One of the key benefits of practicing saying "no" is that it helps you prioritize your own needs and values. It's important to recognize that your time and energy are valuable and should be spent on activities that are meaningful and enjoyable to you. By saying "no" to things that don't align with your values or goals, you can create more balance and fulfillment in your life.

Saying "no" can also help you avoid burnout and maintain your well-being. When you constantly say "yes" to everything, you may find yourself feeling overwhelmed and drained. By setting limits on your time and energy and saying "no" to things that are not a priority, you can protect your own well-being and avoid burnout.

Effective communication is an important part of setting boundaries and saying "no." It's important to be assertive and direct, but also respectful and understanding of others' perspectives. Using "I" statements can help you express your boundaries in a clear and respectful way, while also making it clear that you are expressing your own feelings and needs, rather than trying to control the other person.

It's also important to be consistent in enforcing your boundaries. If you allow someone to cross a boundary one time, it can be confusing and lead to more boundary-pushing in the future.

Tips to Put the Steps into Practice:

Use "I" statements:

1. Express your feelings: Use "I" statements to express how you feel about a particular situation or behavior. For

example, "I feel hurt when you criticize me in front of others."

2. State your needs: Use "I" statements to clearly articulate what you need in a particular situation. For example, "I need some space to process my thoughts before we continue this discussion."

3. Explain the impact of the other person's behavior: Use "I" statements to explain how the other person's behavior has affected you. For example, "I feel disrespected when you interrupt me while I'm speaking."

4. Offer a solution: Use "I" statements to suggest a solution that addresses your feelings and needs. For example, "I would appreciate it if we could discuss this issue when we are both calm and can listen to each other."

Offer an alternative solution:

1. Suggest an alternative time or date: If you are unable to do something at the time it is requested, you can try suggesting an alternative time or date that works better for you.

2. Offer to help in a different way: If you are unable to do something as requested, you can try offering to help in a different way. For example, if you are unable to attend a meeting, you could offer to help by providing notes or summarizing the discussion.

3. Suggest a compromise: If you are unable to do something as requested, you can try suggesting a compromise. For example, if you are unable to work on a project during the weekend, you could offer to work extra hours during the week to make up for it.

4. Refer the person to someone else: If you are unable to do something as requested, you can try referring the person to someone else who may be able to help. This can be a good option if you know someone who has the skills or resources to assist.

Set limits on your time and energy:

1. Create boundaries around your time: Consider setting limits on when you are available to work, socialize, or engage in other activities. For example, you might set a boundary around not working after a certain time in the evening or on weekends.

2. Make a schedule: Creating a schedule can help you prioritize your time and energy. Make a list of the things that are most important to you and schedule time for them. This can help you balance your work, relationships, and personal interests.

3. Learn to say "no": Saying "no" to requests or invitations that don't align with your values or goals can be an effective way to set limits on your time and energy. It's important to be assertive and direct, but also respectful and understanding of others' perspectives.

4. Set limits on your commitments: Consider how many commitments you can realistically handle at any given time. It's okay to say "no" to new commitments if you are already stretched thin.

5. Take breaks: It's important to make time for rest and relaxation. Consider setting limits on your work hours and taking regular breaks throughout the day to recharge.

Use a script:

1. Prepare a script in advance: Take some time to think about what you want to say and write it down. This can help you feel

more confident and prepared when the time comes to say "no."

2. Use "I" statements: Focus on expressing your own feelings and needs, rather than trying to control the other person. For example, instead of saying "You can't do that," try saying "I'm sorry, but I don't feel comfortable with that."

3. Acknowledge the other person's perspective: Show empathy and understanding for the other person's perspective. For example, you could say "I understand that this is important to you, but I have to prioritize my own well-being and I'm unable to take on any additional commitments at this time."

4. Offer an alternative solution: If you don't want to do something, but you don't want to completely shut the other person down, you can try offering an alternative solution. For example, instead of saying "No, I can't work on the weekend," you could say "I can't work on the weekend, but I could work a little extra on Wednesday evening to make up for it."

5. Practice your script: Once you have prepared your script, practice saying it out loud. This can help you feel more comfortable and confident when the time comes to say "no" in a real-life situation.

Practice saying "no" in low-stakes situations:

1. Practice with friends and family: You can practice saying "no" to requests from friends and family members in low-stakes situations. For example, you could practice saying "no" to a friend who asks you to go out when you're feeling tired, or to a family member who asks you to help with a task when you're already busy.

2. Role play with a trusted friend or family member: You can also practice saying "no" by role-playing with a trusted friend or

family member. Set up a scenario and take turns practicing saying "no" in a respectful and assertive way.

3. Practice with a therapist or coach: If you are struggling with saying "no" and would like more support, you can practice with a therapist or coach. They can provide guidance and feedback on how to set and communicate your boundaries effectively.

4. Practice in small ways: You don't have to say "no" to big requests in order to practice this skill. You can start by saying "no" to small requests or invitations that you are not interested in.

Step 5
Enforce Your Boundaries

It's important to follow through with the boundaries you set. If someone violates your boundaries, it's okay to assertively remind them of your boundaries and the consequences of not respecting them.

Enforcing boundaries is an important part of maintaining your personal autonomy and taking care of your mental and emotional well-being. Here are some steps you can follow to help you enforce your boundaries:

1. Identify your boundaries: The first step in enforcing your boundaries is to be aware of what they are. Take some time to think about what you are comfortable with and what you are not comfortable with in different areas of your life, such as your physical space, relationships, communication, and personal time.

2. Communicate your boundaries: Once you have identified your boundaries, it's important to communicate them to others. Be clear and direct about what you are and are not willing to accept or tolerate. You can use "I" statements to express your feelings and needs, such as "I feel overwhelmed when I receive more than three emails in a day" or "I need some time to myself after work."

3. Set limits: If someone crosses your boundaries, it's important to set limits to protect yourself. This could involve saying "no" or setting a boundary around a particular behavior or situation. For example, if someone constantly interrupts you during a conversation, you might say something like "I need to finish what I'm saying before you speak."

4. Practice self-care: Taking care of yourself is an important part of enforcing your boundaries. This might involve setting aside time for activities that help you relax and recharge, such as exercise, meditation, or spending time with friends and family.

5. Seek support: If you are having trouble enforcing your boundaries, it can be helpful to seek support from a trusted friend, family member, or professional therapist. They can offer guidance and help you develop strategies for setting and maintaining your boundaries.

Remember, it's okay to set and enforce boundaries, and it's important to prioritize your own well-being. Don't be afraid to stand up for yourself and advocate for your needs.

Here are some examples of people enforcing their boundaries:

1. A coworker who sets limits on the number of emails they are willing to respond to after hours, and communicates this to their team.

2. A parent who sets boundaries around their personal time and schedules activities with their children accordingly.

3. A friend who sets a boundary around their physical space and asks others to respect their personal space.

4. A partner who sets boundaries around communication and asks for space when they need time to themselves.

5. A person who sets boundaries around their physical safety and refuses to be in situations that make them feel unsafe.

Enforcing boundaries can take many forms and will look different for each person. The important thing is to be clear and assertive about what you are and are not comfortable with, and to take steps to protect your own well-being.

Enforcing your boundaries is a crucial aspect of maintaining your personal autonomy and taking care of your mental and emotional well-being. It involves setting limits around what you are and are not willing to accept or tolerate in different areas of your life, such as your physical space, relationships, communication, and personal time.

One of the main reasons why it's important to enforce your boundaries is that it helps you to protect your own well-being. When you don't set boundaries, you may find yourself in situations that are draining, overwhelming, or even harmful to your physical or emotional health. Setting boundaries allows you to establish healthy limits and take care of yourself, which is essential for your overall well-being.

Another reason why enforcing your boundaries is important is that it helps you to communicate your needs and values to others. When you set boundaries, you are telling others what you are and are not willing to accept or tolerate. This can help you to establish healthy relationships and avoid conflicts that may arise due to misunderstandings or unmet expectations.

In addition to protecting your well-being and communicating your needs, enforcing your boundaries can also help you to develop a stronger sense of self. When you set limits around what you are willing to accept or tolerate, you are taking charge of your own life and making decisions that align with your values and goals. This can help you to build confidence and self-esteem, and feel more in control of your life.

One of the challenges of enforcing your boundaries is that it can be difficult to say "no" or set limits, especially if you are a people-pleaser or tend to avoid conflict. It's important to remember that it's okay to set boundaries and that it's not selfish to prioritize your own well-being. You have the right to establish limits and take care of yourself, and it's important to advocate for your own needs.

Enforcing your boundaries can be a challenging process, but it is an important step in taking care of yourself and establishing healthy relationships. Remember, it's okay to set and enforce boundaries, and it's important to prioritize your own well-being. Don't be afraid to stand up for yourself and advocate for your needs. It's important to remember that enforcing your boundaries doesn't mean that you have to be rigid or inflexible. It's okay to be open to compromise and to make exceptions when necessary, but it's important to do so in a way that still respects your own needs and boundaries.

One of the key things to remember when enforcing your boundaries is to be assertive, not aggressive. Assertiveness involves standing up for your own rights and needs in a way that is respectful of others, while aggression involves violating the rights of others. It's important to be clear and direct when setting boundaries, but it's also important to do so in a way that doesn't hurt or disrespect others.

Finally, it's important to remember that enforcing your boundaries is a continuous process. It's something that you will need to work on throughout your life, as your boundaries may change and evolve over time. It's important to be open to learning and growing, and to be willing to adjust your boundaries as needed to align with your changing needs and values.

Tips to Put the Steps into Practice:

Identify your boundaries:

1. Reflect on your values: Your boundaries may be influenced by your personal values and beliefs. Take some time to think about what is important to you and how you want to live your life. This can help you to identify the areas where you want to set boundaries.

2. Notice your physical and emotional reactions: Pay attention to your physical and emotional reactions to different situations. Do you feel overwhelmed, drained, or disrespected in certain situations? These reactions can be clues that you need to set a boundary.

3. Consider your past experiences: Think about past experiences where you felt uncomfortable or violated. What were the circumstances that led to these feelings? How could you have set a boundary to prevent these situations from occurring in the future?

4. Seek feedback from trusted friends and family: Ask trusted friends and family members for their perspective on your boundaries. They may be able to offer insights and help you to identify areas where you may need to set limits.

5. Consult with a therapist: If you are having difficulty identifying your boundaries, a therapist can be a helpful resource. They can help you to explore your feelings and needs and assist you in setting and enforcing healthy boundaries.

Communicate your boundaries:

1. Use "I" statements: When communicating your boundaries, it's important to use "I" statements that express your feelings and needs. For example, instead of saying "You always interrupt me," you might say "I feel disrespected when I'm

interrupted." This helps to convey your perspective without blaming or judging the other person.

2. Be clear and direct: It's important to be clear and direct when communicating your boundaries. Use specific language to describe what you are and are not willing to accept or tolerate. For example, instead of saying "I don't like it when you do that," you might say "I don't feel comfortable when you do that, and I need you to stop."

3. Set limits: If someone crosses your boundaries, it's important to set limits to protect yourself. This could involve saying "no" or setting a boundary around a particular behavior or situation. For example, if someone constantly interrupts you during a conversation, you might say something like "I need to finish what I'm saying before you speak."

4. Practice assertiveness: Assertiveness involves standing up for your own rights and needs in a way that is respectful of others. It's important to be assertive when communicating your boundaries, as this helps to convey your perspective and needs without violating the rights of others.

5. Seek support: If you are having trouble communicating your boundaries, it can be helpful to seek support from a trusted friend, family member, or professional therapist. They can offer guidance and help you develop strategies for setting and maintaining your boundaries.

Set limits:

1. Say "no": One of the most effective ways to set limits is to simply say "no" when you are not comfortable with a particular request or situation. It's important to be firm and clear when saying "no," and to avoid making excuses or apologetic statements.

2. Set boundaries around specific behaviors: If there is a specific behavior that is crossing your boundaries, you can set a

boundary around that behavior. For example, if someone is constantly interrupting you during a conversation, you might say something like "I need to finish what I'm saying before you speak."

3. Set limits on your time and energy: You can also set limits on your time and energy by setting boundaries around how much of your time and energy you are willing to give to others. This might involve setting limits on how often you are available or how much you are willing to take on.

4. Seek support: If you are having trouble setting limits, it can be helpful to seek support from a trusted friend, family member, or professional therapist. They can offer guidance and help you develop strategies for setting and maintaining your boundaries.

Practice self-care:

1. Exercise and physical activity: Engaging in physical activity can help to reduce stress, improve mood, and boost energy levels. It can be as simple as taking a walk or going for a run, or you can try more structured activities like yoga or lifting weights.

2. Eating a healthy diet: Taking care of your body by fueling it with nourishing foods can help to improve your overall health and well-being. This might involve eating a balanced diet that includes a variety of fruits, vegetables, whole grains, and lean proteins.

3. Getting enough sleep: Sleep is essential for physical and mental health. Make sure to get enough sleep each night by establishing a consistent bedtime routine and creating a sleep-friendly environment.

4. Taking breaks and relaxing: It's important to take breaks and relax in order to recharge your batteries. This might involve

activities like reading, watching a movie, or spending time with friends and family.

5. Engaging in activities that you enjoy: Doing things that you enjoy can help to reduce stress and improve your mood. This might involve hobbies, creative pursuits, or other activities that bring you joy and relaxation.

6. Seeking support: Sometimes it can be helpful to talk to someone about your feelings and struggles. This might involve seeking support from a trusted friend or family member, or seeking the help of a professional therapist.

Seek support:

1. Talk to a trusted friend or family member: Sharing your feelings and struggles with someone you trust can be a helpful way to get support and perspective.

2. Seek the help of a professional therapist: A therapist can offer guidance and support as you work on enforcing your boundaries. They can also help you to identify any underlying issues that may be impacting your ability to set and maintain boundaries.

3. Join a support group: Joining a support group, either in-person or online, can be a great way to connect with others who are also working on setting and enforcing their boundaries.

4. Use self-help resources: There are many self-help books and online resources available that can provide guidance and support as you work on enforcing your boundaries.

5. Practice self-care: Taking care of yourself is an important part of enforcing your boundaries. This might involve setting aside time for activities that help you relax and recharge, such as exercise, meditation, or spending time with friends and family.

Step 6
Be Consistent

It's important to be consistent in enforcing your boundaries. If you allow someone to cross a boundary one time, it can be confusing and lead to more boundary-pushing in the future.

Consistency is important in many areas of life, including setting and enforcing boundaries. Here are some steps you can follow to help you be consistent:

1. Identify your values and priorities: The first step in being consistent is to be clear about what is important to you. Take some time to think about your values and priorities, and make sure that your actions and decisions align with these.

2. Set clear goals: Setting specific and achievable goals can help you to stay focused and on track. Make sure to set both short-term and long-term goals, and be specific about what you want to accomplish.

3. Make a plan: Once you have identified your goals, make a plan for how you will achieve them. This might involve breaking your goals down into smaller, more manageable tasks, and setting deadlines for each one.

4. Stay organized: Being organized can help you to stay on top of your tasks and responsibilities, and make it easier to stay consistent. This might involve using tools like a calendar, to-do list, or planner to help you stay organized.

5. Be flexible: While it's important to be consistent, it's also important to be flexible and open to change. Make sure to leave room for adjustments and be willing to make adjustments as needed.

6. Seek support: If you are having trouble being consistent, it can be helpful to seek support from a trusted friend, family member, or professional therapist. They can offer guidance and help you develop strategies for staying consistent.

Remember, being consistent is an important aspect of achieving your goals and maintaining healthy relationships. It takes time and effort, but the benefits are worth it. With practice and patience, you can develop consistent habits and achieve your goals.

Here are some examples of people who are consistent with the boundaries they set:

1. A person who consistently sets limits around their personal time and communicates this to their friends and family, such as by setting aside certain times for self-care or saying "no" to social invitations when they need time to themselves.

2. A parent who consistently sets boundaries around their children's behavior and follows through with consequences when those boundaries are violated.

3. A coworker who consistently communicates their expectations and limits around work-related tasks and responsibilities, such as by setting clear deadlines or delegating tasks as needed.

4. A friend who consistently sets boundaries around their physical space and communicates this to others, such as by asking others to respect their personal space or setting limits around how much time they are willing to spend with certain people.

5. A person who consistently sets boundaries around their physical safety and communicates this to others, such as by refusing to be in situations that make them feel unsafe or by setting limits around physical contact.

Consistency is an important aspect of setting and enforcing boundaries. When you are consistent with the boundaries you set, it helps others to understand what you are and are not willing to accept or tolerate, and it can help to establish healthy and respectful relationships.

One of the main benefits of being consistent with your boundaries is that it helps to establish trust and respect. When you are consistent in the boundaries you set, others know what to expect from you and can trust that you will follow through with your limits. This can help to build strong and healthy relationships, as it allows others to feel safe and respected.

Another reason why consistency is important with boundaries is that it helps to prevent misunderstandings and conflicts. When you are consistent in the boundaries you set, it helps to avoid misunderstandings and miscommunications, as others know what to expect from you. This can help to prevent conflicts and misunderstandings, as others know what is and is not acceptable.

In addition to establishing trust and preventing misunderstandings, consistency with boundaries can also help to protect your own well-being. When you are consistent in the boundaries you set, you are taking charge of your own life and making decisions that align with your values and goals. This can help you to feel more in control of your life and can contribute to your overall well-being.

One of the challenges of being consistent with your boundaries is that it can be difficult to stick to your limits, especially if you are a people-pleaser or tend to avoid conflict. It's important to remember that it's okay to set boundaries and that it's not selfish to prioritize your own well-being. You have the right to establish limits and take care of yourself, and it's important to advocate for your own needs.

Tips to Put the Steps into Practice:

Make a plan:

1. Determine your goal: The first step in making a plan is to identify what you want to achieve. This could be a short-term goal, such as preparing for a presentation, or a long-term goal, such as saving for retirement. Be specific and clear about what you want to accomplish.

2. Break down your goal into smaller steps: Once you have identified your goal, it can be helpful to break it down into smaller, more manageable steps. This can make the goal feel more achievable and help you stay focused.

3. Establish a timeline: Establishing a timeline can help you stay on track and make progress towards your goal. Consider setting deadlines for each of the smaller steps you have identified, as well as a final deadline for achieving your overall goal.

4. Gather resources: Consider what resources you will need in order to achieve your goal. This could include things like information, materials, or support from others. Make a list of the resources you will need and consider how you can obtain them.

5. Make a schedule: Creating a schedule can help you stay organized and ensure that you have dedicated time to work on your goal. Consider blocking out specific times on your calendar to work on your goal, and try to stick to your schedule as closely as possible.

6. Review and adjust your plan: As you work towards your goal, it's important to regularly review your progress and make adjustments as needed. This might involve revising your timeline, adjusting your schedule, or gathering additional resources.

Stay organized:

1. prioritize tasks and stay on track. Consider using a planner or a digital tool like Google Calendar or Trello to keep track of your tasks and appointments.

2. Set aside dedicated work or study time: Setting aside specific times of the day or week for work or study can help you to stay focused and avoid getting sidetracked.

3. Use an organizational system: Using an organizational system, such as folders, labels, or bins, can help you to keep your papers, documents, and other items organized and easy to find.

4. Create a designated workspace: Having a dedicated workspace can help you to stay focused and organized. Consider setting up a desk or work area that is free from distractions and clutter.

5. Get rid of unnecessary items: Getting rid of items that you no longer need or use can help to declutter your space and make it easier to stay organized. Consider doing a regular decluttering session or using the "one in, one out" rule to keep things in check.

6. Follow a routine: Establishing a regular routine can help you to stay organized and on track. Consider setting aside time for tasks like meal planning, grocery shopping, and cleaning on a regular basis.

REMINDER 1: While it's important to be consistent, it's also important to be open to adjusting your boundaries when necessary. For example, if you have a boundary around not working on weekends, but a deadline comes up that requires you to work on a Saturday, it may be necessary to adjust your boundary in this situation.

REMINDER 2: Setting and maintaining boundaries can be draining, so it's important to make sure you are taking care of yourself. This may involve making time for self-care activities, such as exercise, meditation, or hobbies.

REMINDER 3: It can be helpful to have a support system of friends and family members who can help you set and maintain healthy boundaries. Talk to them about your boundaries and ask for their help in enforcing them.

Wrapping it Up

As we navigated the challenges of setting and enforcing boundaries, we learned the importance of identifying your own needs and values. By taking the time to reflect on what was most important to you, we learned to set limits and establish healthy boundaries in our relationships and in lives.

We also learned the value of clear and effective communication. By using "I" statements and being assertive, to be able to express your needs and boundaries in a way that is respectful and effective.

We also discovered the importance of self-awareness. By paying attention to our own thoughts and feelings, we're able to identify when our boundaries are being crossed and take action to protect ourselves.

Saying "no" is another crucial aspect of setting boundaries for us. We learned that it's okay to set limits and that it's not selfish to prioritize our own well-being.

Enforcing our boundaries and being consistent were also important components. We learned that it's essential to be clear and direct about our limits, and to follow through on the boundaries we set.

The journey of setting and enforcing boundaries, is a transformative process. We become more confident, self-assured, and in control of our own lives. Setting and enforcing boundaries is an ongoing process, yet rewarding to continue on the journey and take care of ourselves in a way that aligns with our own needs and values.

Thank you for taking the time to read this book on setting boundaries. I hope that the tips and strategies we provided were helpful in helping you identify your needs and communicate them clearly. I also hope that you have gained a greater understanding of the importance of self-awareness and the power of saying "no" in order to protect your own well-being.

Additionally, I hope that you have learned the value of enforcing your boundaries and being consistent in maintaining them. By following these principles, you can build healthier and more fulfilling relationships with others, as well as with yourself.

Again, I am grateful that you chose to read our book and hope that it has provided you with the tools you need to set and maintain strong boundaries in your life.

YOU

VS

BOUNDARIES

A Step-By-Step Guide to Setting Healthy Boundaries to Take Control of Your Life

By: Dominic Cooper